Ten P
about B

ex libris

Candlestick Press

Published by:
Candlestick Press,
Diversity House, 72 Nottingham Road, Arnold, Nottingham UK NG5 6LF
www.candlestickpress.co.uk

Design and typesetting by Diversity Creative Marketing Solutions Ltd.,
www.diversity.agency

Printed by Ratcliff & Roper Print Group, Nottinghamshire, UK

Selection © Di Slaney, 2017

Cover illustration © Hilke MacIntyre, 2017 www.hilke.macintyre-art.com

Candlestick Press monogram © Barbara Shaw, 2008

© Candlestick Press, 2017

ISBN 978 1 907598 49 4

Acknowledgements:

The poems in this pamphlet are reprinted from the following books, all by
permission of the publishers listed unless stated otherwise. Every effort has
been made to trace the copyright holders of the poems published in this
book. The editor and publisher apologise if any material has been included
without permission or without the appropriate acknowledgement, and
would be glad to be told of anyone who has not been consulted. Thanks are
due to all the copyright holders cited below for their kind permission:

Matthew Dickman and Michael Dickman, *Brother* (Faber & Faber, 2016)

Jonathan Edwards, *My Family and Other Superheroes* (Seren, 2014) by
permission of the publisher

Lavinia Greenlaw, *Minsk* (Faber & Faber, 2004)

Joanne Limburg, *The Autistic Alice* (Bloodaxe Books, 2017),
www.bloodaxebooks.com

Hannah Lowe, *Chick* (Bloodaxe Books, 2013), www.bloodaxebooks.com

Rebecca McClanahan, *Deep Light: New and Selected Poems*,
1987-2007 (Iris Books, 2007)

Rob Miles, poem as yet unpublished, by kind permission of the author

Mary O'Donnell, *Those April Fevers* (Arc Publications, 2015)

Ben Scammell, in *New Lake Poets*, ed. William Scammell (Bloodaxe
Books, 1991) by kind permission of the author

Floyd Skloot, 'The Everly Brothers' first appeared in *Prairie Schooner*
Vol. 65. No. 3 (Fall, 1991) by permission of University of Nebraska Press

All permissions cleared courtesy of Swift Permissions
(swiftpermissions@gmail.com)

Contents

Brothers

You know the sort: they borrow each other's t-shirts,
wear each other's sweat under their armpits.
In the pub, you swear you hear one's voice and turn
to find the other chatting up your girl,
or else you catch one, curling up his lip,
as if he's trying on his brother's smile,
or you go to the bar and they both show up.
One has a knackered Transit, the other jump leads.
They've one gym membership and their own bodies,
tell the punch lines to each other's jokes
and if you're fool enough to bother one,
you'll find yourself outside with both of them.
You know the sort: the elder has a child
who's got her mother's mouth, her uncle's eyes.

Jonathan Edwards

Fist

When my brother put his fist through a window
on New Year's Eve, no one noticed until a cold draft
cooled our bodies dancing. There was rainbow light
from a disco ball, silver tinsel round the pictures.
My brother held his arm out to us, palm
upturned, a foot high spray of blood.
This was Ilford, Essex, 1993, nearly midnight,
us all smashed on booze and Ecstasy and Danny,
6 foot 5, folding at the knee, a shiny fin of glass
wedged in his wrist. We walked him to the kitchen,
the good arm slung on someone's neck,
Gary shouting *Danny*, Darren phoning
for an ambulance, the blood was everywhere. I pressed
a towel across the wound, around the glass
and led him by the hand into the garden, he stumbled
down into the snow, slurring *leave it out* and *I'm OK*.
A girl was crying in the doorway, the music carried on,
the bass line thumping as we stood around my brother,
Gary talking gently saying *easy fella*, Darren
draining Stella in one hand and in the other, holding up
my brother's arm, wet and red, the veins stood out
like branches. I thought that he was dying,
out there in the snow and I got down, I knelt there
on the ice and held my brother, who I never touched
and never told I loved, and even then I couldn't say it
so I listened to the incantation *easy fella*
and my brother's breathing,

felt him rolling forward, all that weight, Darren
throwing down his can and yelling *Danny, don't you dare*
and shaking him. My brother's face was grey,
his lips were loose and pale and I
was praying. Somewhere in the street,
there was a siren, there was a girl inside
who blamed herself, there were men with blankets
and a tourniquet, they stopped my brother bleeding,
as the New Year turned, they saved him,
snow was falling hard, they saved us all.

Hannah Lowe

More Than One Life

My older brother is standing outside the movie theater like a man
I have never met. Standing in the snow, looking up
at posters for films
that haven't played in over fifty years. In this dream
he's thirteen years old
and then he's thirty, and then he's nothing. John Wayne
is looking down at him and so is Greta Garbo. Here in New York
Marlene Dietrich is inhaling all the death
a close-up can gather in its big, beautiful, hazy arms. My brother
has lit a cigarette.
He's turning up his collar.
He looks like Gary Cooper. He flicks the butt into the street
like a detective, his long fingers making a shadow
across the sidewalk. In this life
nothing inside him wants to pull a knife, load a gun, open a package
of pain killers. In this life he has a day off
and is going to see a movie and buy some popcorn and sit in a darkness
he can rise from, and walk up the aisle like a groom, walk
out into the air again, and down the street, and whistle maybe, and
      go home.

Matthew Dickman

Ex-Brother-in-Law

Without the law, there is no brother,
and no ceremony to mark the breaking.
Christmas Eve from the box packed away last year
we uncover the stocking stitched with your name,
not knowing what to do with it. Later as we gather
to watch family slides projected on a sheet,
your face surfaces among ours, miraculous
as the imprints emerging on the shroud of Turin.
When you were here, how simple it seemed,
the pattern of blame and solution: If only you would turn
that way or this, if only you would disappear,
my sister's life could begin again. But what of *our* lives,
the severed sisters, aunts, brothers, nephews, nieces,
fathers, mothers – all those unregistered
couplings of hearts – left to wonder
if you were ever ours, and by what decree.

Have you married some new family, are you sharing
their holiday feast while we sit here
at the table you refinished – your windburnt hands
with the freckled knuckles, rough-hewn hands
that sanded until the grain revealed itself,
the complicated whorls beneath the surface
where so much of you remains: The daughter
you started fourteen years ago wears your face
and keeps growing. And your son still brags
about the time you accidentally shot a power-driven
nail through your hand while building
a skate ramp – *For me!* he sings proudly. *For me!*

Rebecca McClanahan

For us, brother

it was all fists and sun, who could take it
or have to break away. Hands down
as kids it was torture

tournaments on hot car bonnets, or tarry
prints on everything from digging up
the brand new path

for loaded games with giant farmyard steel
wheel bearings, or my vision
cobwebbed in an instant

on that garden chipping freed and
ricocheting from your new Black Widow
catapult, then my steady nails,

in thoughtful retribution, pushing
through the taut tissue on the body
of your balsa wood planes, or our small palms

crossed with heated coppers
as we scrapped for scalding pennies
scattered at the fair around the old

town crier's boots, or scoring broken Bic
tattoos with still-stinging quills
around shadow, knuckle

and spasm, or flint-sharp sticks swiping
at the lucky tracer sparks
whirling in a storm of dirty light

behind a tractor on its tilting
lap of honour, fuming past us holding up
its torch of cooling hay.

Rob Miles

The Everly Brothers

My brother thought they were freaks
of nature, voices fitting together
through some fluke of chemistry.
He said they might just as well
have been Siamese twins sharing
a heart or the Everly humpbacks.

My brother preferred Jerry
Lee Lewis and Chuck Berry.
He cackled at their antics,
battering mother's baby
grand with his fists when we
were alone and duckwalking
the hallway until our downstairs
neighbors hit their ceiling
with a broom. At night he worked
on his Elvis sneer while caking
his face with Clearasil.

I can still see my brother
rave as we rode four stories
up in the quaking elevator.
He offered me one frenzied
groove of Yakety Yak at the top
of his lungs when I tried
to sing. All I wanted was
his voice joining mine in
harmony. The song did not
have to be about faith in love.

Floyd Skloot

The Spirit of the Staircase

In our game of flight, half-way down
was as near mid-air as it got: a point
of no return we'd fling ourselves at
over and over, riding pillows or trays.
We were quick to smooth the edge
of every step, grinding the carpet to glass
on which we'd lose our grip.
The new stairs were our new toy,
the descent to an odd extension,
four new rooms at flood level
in a sunken garden – a wing
dislocated from a hive. Young bees
with soft stripes and borderless nights,
we'd so far been squared away
in a twin-set of bunkbeds, so tight-knit,
my brother and I once woke up finishing
a conversation begun in a dream.
It had been the simplest exchange,
one I'd give much to return to:
the greetings of shadows unsurprised
at having met beneath the trees
and happy to set off again, alone,
back into the dark.

Lavinia Greenlaw

Brother

'Hi,' you said, whenever I picked up: your name
was never asked for. Of course I knew your name.

I can't unknow it now, and you can't make me.
I bagsied it, I chew on it; your name

is ever imminent on my tongue. I start
to talk about my son, but use your name

instead, run two names together just
like Dad would muddle ours – mynameyourname –

as if he had one composite child. Two 'J's,
two final 'n's – we nearly shared a name.

Now I'm Joanne, alone, and call your name.
For pity's sake, pick up.

Joanne Limburg

A Boy in Gaza

Will he remember how his sister dragged him
from the street just after the explosion,

how, running, she carried him through rubble?
Eyes wide, her legs stretched in flight

as she leaped across smashed melons, pulped figs
and open-mouthed, still faces. In the photo, her brother's

trousers are stained with blood splatters,
dust, her hair is a nest above her ears, grey

with exploded particles. One arm clenches
his small body against her hip as she

races for their lives, agile
as a fleeing deer from a flaming forest,

her right foot frozen forever, poised in flight,
not yet grounded as she avoids

broken dervishes of mothers, men bawling
like beasts for one another, for their children.

She avoids too the flown daggers of wood
that could pinion her flesh or his

if she puts one foot wrong.
Will he remember his fleeing sister?

Mary O'Donnell

My Lost Brother

And last but not least, my own brother –
who has made, out of petrol and hormones,

a little world for himself, a paradise
of hang-gliders and cars;

where he is clearly recognisable
as himself,

swung in mid-air
above a hill-side.

He has gone to Switzerland
to take in the sights

working his way back
through his own hard-won youth,

its easy roundabouts and hard spring ground;
his world rolled tight as a sleeping-bag.

Ben Scammell